D1365461

an infatuation

Golf

by David Baird
Illustrations by Anny Evason

M·Q·P

Do you golf? Whether you do or not, this little companion book will help you to come to terms with the most wonderful, strange, fanatical and addictive sport imaginable. The terms, facts, stories, jokes, anecdotes and tips found here can be pleasingly mixed with your own recordings and dragged out to suit the occasion. Male or female, young or old, don't go out into 'tiger country' without this volume and make certain before you give that company speech or host a dinner party that you consult these pages … they could just save the day!

What is it about knocking a little white ball around the countryside with expensive and strange-looking sticks, often dressed up like a ninny and despite the worst weather imaginable, that makes golf so blooming popular? The heartaches and triumphs are extreme, the prizes phenomenal, the side-bets are many and the kudos great. Imagine the extent of the business being carried out on golf courses throughout the world at this very minute.

Don't count in anything less than billions! Then there's the books, the merchandise, the television franchises, the club houses, the sponsorship deals, why there's even a megamillion counterfeit business offering copied clubs, bags ...you name it.

Golf is much more than a game, it's an entire world complete with its deals and rivalry, espionage, sabotage and, perhaps most importantly of all and the factor that separates the golfer from the ordinary world, is that golf has its very own complex, almost seductive language, without which you won't get far from that first little pointy whatsit that the ball sits on before you hit it with the longer stick thingy with the dumpy bit on the end and the wrapping on the handle...Oh, yes, the tee!

A is for Ace...
Or in other words a hole in one…

A is for Address...

Don't forget to address the ball. No, I don't mean to suggest that you're going to hit it so far that it will need to be mailed back. It means to take up your stance and prepare yourself to hit the ball. Simple, you would think, but nothing in golf is straightforward. Somewhere in the rules it is written that the player has addressed the ball when the stance has been taken and the player has also grounded the club. But then, in a 'hazard' a player is considered to have addressed the ball the moment the stance has been taken. Now…imagine you've placed your ball on the tee and it falls off whilst the player is addressing it. Well, many eyebrows will become raised and a complex investigation will begin to ascertain whether in fact it was caused by anything whatsoever the player might have done during the address.

Still on the subject of the 'address', this is also the moment that distinguishes every player and leaves a television viewer perplexed by the unusual habits and customs of the golfing fraternity. Why? Because it is at this point that coaching recommends forming the habit of wiggling once or twice…no, not as a mating ritual, although it's well known that golfers, professional and amateur, are frequently seen accompanied by attractive partners…Still, like some peculiar courting dance performed by the blue-footed booby, players place themselves on view to the entire world and waggle their stuff. It can be messy, certainly off-putting, but for the player doing the waggling it'll get rid of a string of imperfections and allow them to carry out the task of whacking that pill as positively as they can at that moment.

A is for Air shot...

For the player involved this is perhaps as embarrassing as meeting the Queen and discovering, whilst your head is bowed, that the pair of knickers you rolled up in your trousers is now hanging out from the turn-up and sitting spats-like on your shoe. Of course, air shot means to miss the ball entirely with your stroke. W C Fields had a quick retort for this occasion, which went something like, 'It's the best stroke I've made all day!' Many friends won't count air shots and, if you find yourself on the 18th standing all square with the chairman of a large Japanese corporation you are trying to get a signature from and he makes an air shot, I'm sure you'll make the right decision about whether or not to count it! Best thing, perhaps, is to fake a heart attack then and there and concede the game.

A is for Albatross...

Nothing to do with the Ancient Mariner but a bird to be kind to all the same. Sometimes referred to also as a double-eagle, it is of course a term used for 'holing out' in three strokes under par for a hole, ie, on a par five hole, you go down in two shots. Nice going! Jack Nicklaus apparently has only ever had three albatrosses in his entire career. The third only happened to him in 1996 during the third round of the Tradition (which he went on to win) in Scottsdale, Arizona, placing 31 years between that and the albatross he got at the Jacksonville Open in 1965.

A is for Amateur...
Not to be confused with the 'duffer', which we'll go
into later.

The 'amateur' – a tricky subject this one and has been
for well over a century, although these days the ruling
is far clearer. Until recently, if you so much as sold your golf
clubs or were given a free hotel room or bus ticket you
would not be able to define yourself as an amateur.
Nowadays amateur status is defined as applying to anyone
who plays the game for no remuneration whatsoever and
who does not stand to profit from the game. Going back to
that encounter with the Japanese chairman and the potential
bonus attached to closing the deal from your end, I'd check
if I were you before entering into any scenario that might
threaten your prized ranking as an amateur. Bother the
chairman of your club or the people in the pro shop with this
one...it makes for an interesting conversation. Remember
that to be an amateur does not mean to be incompetent or
unskilful as a player, it's all to do with profit.

A is for Architecture...

What is green, narrow, shorter than the fairway but not as short as the green whilst surrounding it?
An apron.

All part of golf's architecture. There is a wonderful quote attributed to Howard O'Brien about the architect of Pebble Beach whom, he said, must have derived his inspiration for the course from Dante's account of a journey through Hell! There are probably few courses you can think of whose architecture would qualify for this description. Perhaps it is for this reason that the term 'attack' came into being. Players go out onto the course expecting to attack each hole in a different way. Suddenly it's war! (But try to avoid the bunkers…)

Notes

B is for Back...
How's your back?

The term 'back' appears everywhere. You can play a hole at its longest distance by teeing off from the back tees. It's also the term used for the 10th to 18th holes (the back nine holes…with the clubhouse bar being the 19th hole. Mine's a whiskey!) Confused? Then how about your backstroke, which is really your backswing and is that place where you swing your club back to reach the point where your downswing comes into play.

B is for Baff...
Baffled?

Then rest easy and let's paint a picture. Imagine a word that represents a blow made with something soft. Try banging the table with a rolled newspaper or a tea towel and listen to the sound carefully. There, did you hear 'baff'? It's a wonderful old Scottish term which Peter Davies in his golfing dictionary traces back to the Flemish *baf,* 'a slap in the face'. What it actually refers to in golf is a stroke where the club-head must 'baff' the ground behind the ball in order to obtain elevation without distance.

Not to be confused with the 'baffy', a club no longer in use (also known as the number 4), a steeply lofted wood with a small head. P G Wodehouse was known to take a 'baffy' for his second after a good tee shot.

Not to be confused with the 'duffer'. The 'duffer' is the quaint term given to the incompetent, unskilled player…perhaps the Sunday only player, hence the 'Sunday duffer' of which there are millions worldwide, all getting out to the course hours before their turn to play arrives, all absolutely fascinated by the game.

Imagine the conversation so far…'Yes, I shot an albatross on the back nine when a duffer with a baffy cut a right hand dog-leg over the hog-back to make the perfect approach on a fine-looking apron.'

Hmmm! Catching on?

B is for Bad-tempered...

I can't tell you how often I've seen balls knocked out of bounds or into traps by careless golfers...particularly the bad-tempered golfer...you know the sort. The person who slices on the first tee and then gets progressively angrier and angrier with every shot until the entire game is wasted. No chance of a bail out. Hey fool...watch a pro. Jack Nicklaus, Tony Jacklin, even Lee Travino. These players concentrate and continue to compete even when things don't go their way. You might as well quit now if you're going to carry the extra baggage of every fluffed shot through the entire 18 holes.

B is for Ball...

The golf ball itself is a curiosity of no little interest. Because of its need to be hard and resiliant, this fascinating (and collectable) projectile has over the centuries been made of wood, of compressed wool in a leather casing, boiled and then compressed feathers, again in a leather casing, solid gutta percha, strip rubber wound around a core with a balata casing (derived from the gum of the bully or balata tree), solid compressed synthetic rubber and, today with hundreds of indentations on its surface. According to the Rules of the Royal & Ancient Golf Club of St Andrews, Scotland, the ball shall not exceed a weight of 45.93gm and the size shall not be less than 41.15mm in diameter.

Listed in the Accounts of the Lords High Treasurers of Scotland in 1506 is: 'Item for xii golf ballis to the King... 4 shillings.'

It is interesting to note that in 1823 the employment of ball making was accounted as being unhealthy, with many ball makers being observed to 'fall sacrifice to consumption'.

Notes

B is for Ball marker...

Beware the unscrupulous ball marker who will cunningly mark his ball from the front before lifting it and who will then replace the ball to the front of the marker, thus making his ball closer to the hole. There are numerous comments to be passed to such opportunists, such as, 'You'll hole that before you even touch your putter', or, disguising the remark within the topic of the weather, 'Close, isn't it!' to which a partner might add, 'Yes, and getting even closer!'

B is for Ball of fire...

Apparently, one day in 1959 it was a sweltering 100 degrees fahrenheit plus, when a golfer in Baltimore drove off from the tee...His ball literally began to burn up mid-flight and the debris fell to earth to start a grass fire! Now that you know about this you will undoubtedly run off and attempt to become a red-hot golfer yourself...hopefully not a pyromaniac!

B is for Bunker...

Many golfers would not have been surprised to receive over the radio news that a certain Mr Hitler killed himself in his bunker! Many a keen golfer, finding themselves in a bunker, would like to do the same. But, of course, the bunkers we refer to here are prepared hazards on the golf course where the ground has been hollowed out, deturfed and replaced with sand etc. Remember, you've addressed the ball once you've taken your stance in the bunker and you mustn't ground the club!

Notes

B is for Body-language...

Tom Lehman says that, even if Seve Ballesteros were to hit a shot 100 yards off line his body language would be saying:

'Hey, if you don't watch the next shot you're going to miss the greatest shot ever hit!'

C is for Caddie...

I was a 'caddie' as a boy and spent as much time in 'tiger-country' with the other urchins seeking out lost balls between rounds as I did toting bags for the 'tigers'. But I can still remember some wonderful professional and amateur players as well as quite a large number of flashy no-hopers out to impress and failing miserably. Yes, the 'duffers'.

I've never really had the time to 'play' the game properly myself, although I've been fortunate enough to have started many tournaments involving pro's and am's at some of the nicest courses imaginable around the world. I've watched them play and heard them talking. My own interest in the game has led me to participate on occasion in the more dedicated players' practice sessions, either by helping to video their swing or simply by collecting hundreds of practice balls. For me, watching good golf is probably more inspiring than playing poor golf myself and here are a few observations that perhaps you'll agree with and which might help your game.

C is for Caddies...

It's a sad fact that the oversized, overkitted golfer always seems to end up picking the skinniest, weakest-looking caddie and insists upon weighing him down with enough excess baggage to ground a Jumbo jet. One such fairway fashion victim, about 100 yards from the green, was heard to call to her scrawny caddie, 'Do you think I can get home with my 7 iron?'

The poor little guy threw up his shoulders and replied, 'Lady, I don't even know where you live!'

Notes

C is for Concentration...

Treat each shot equally from the outset. Tell yourself that you're going to give every single stroke your complete concentration and give it your very best attempt. If you approach a stroke half-heartedly you certainly can't expect a good result. Watch some great players and you'll see it works. Good examples are Jack Nicklaus, Tony Jacklin and the comedian Jimmy Tarbuck, whose low handicap is the proof of the pudding.

Notes

C is for Car parks

It was in the car park at Gleneagles. A priest was coming outside when he spotted a frail-looking elderly gentleman standing at the rear of an estate car, surrounded by golfing bags, suitcases and all the trimmings. The priest felt a glow of goodwill, strode over to the car and with a smile to the older fellow declared, 'We'll soon have these clubs loaded, don't you worry!' In all, it took only a matter of a minute or so for the agile young priest to load the entire ensemble into the rear of the car.

'There,' he said, brushing his hands together in several light claps.

'That's very kind of you, father,' said the elderly man, 'but my son is going to be extremely annoyed, I fear.'

'What on earth for?' exclaimed the priest. 'Is your son such a tyrant that he expects his aged father to do all the heavy work?'

'No.' replied the man. 'It's just that he was in the back of the car trying to find his glasses when you came along and buried him alive!'

C is for Clubs...

I heard a joke many years ago and can't remember who told it or exactly how it went, but it's something like this…A rich oil sheikh had commissioned a top-ranking British engineer to design and construct a new dam on his territory. It was a vital project for the sheikh and the future of his lands and people.

This engineer succeeded in completing the job in less time than originally projected and came in bang on cost. It was a magnificent feat and the sheikh was much impressed with the engineer's achievement. So much so that he arranged for a casket of beautiful gems to be presented to the man along with his substantial fee. The man handed back the casket to the bemused sheikh and said; 'Thank you very much but I can't accept these. I am extremely glad that you are happy with my work and my fee is reward enough.'

The sheikh shrugged his shoulders and ordered the casket be taken away. He then reached into his clothing and produced a diamond, the likes of which only Liz Taylor will have ever seen before and thrust it into the engineer's hand but, as soon as he felt its arrival, the engineer handed it back to the now-concerned sheikh.

'My dear fellow,' he said to the engineer, 'if you do not allow me to present you with a gift, as is my custom, I shall be extremely offended.'

The engineer scratched his chin in thought. 'I'm sorry, I wasn't aware that I was offending you. There is something you could give to me that I would accept', he said.

The sheikh, delighted asked, 'What is it? Anything at all, you name it and it shall be yours.'

'I'm a keen golfer,' the engineer began, 'and I could use a couple of new golf clubs. You could get them for me and we'll both be happy.' The sheikh agreed and they parted on good terms.

Back in England several weeks later a solicitor knocked on the engineer's door.

'Sir,' began the solicitor, 'the sheikh has asked me to carry out his wishes regarding your golf clubs. He has selected and purchased three for you. He apologises that only two of them have swimming pools but the one in Scotland has wonderful shooting!'

C is for Courses...

To list all the worthy golf courses in the world would take several thick volumes and six lifetimes of research (and that's only if you start at age six and get up at 5:30am to start playing every day!).

Florida on its own has well over 1100 golf courses (not to mention Daytona Beach, Cypress Knoll, Indigo Lakes...) so I'm merely going to whet the appetite and you're going to search out a little paradise of your own somewhere in the world at a later date. There are plenty of good golf guides published to help you out.

Without a doubt the home of golf and the rules by which to play it is the Royal & Ancient Golf Club of St Andrews in Scotland. Ask any player. But then what about the wonderful Gleneagles in Auchterarder. This boasts the King's Course (moorland), 6125 yards par 69, and the Queen's Course (moorland), 5660 yards par 67. Also the Monarch's Course and, at nine holes, the Wee Course, 1481 yards par 27. I personally love the Manor House Hotel and Golf Course in Moretonhampstead, set in parkland on the edge of Dartmoor National Park, 18 holes over 6016 yards S S S (Standard Scratch Score) 69. If you like sea and sand dunes then Harlech or Porthcawl in Wales are wonderfully atmospheric and challenging courses. But now I'm stuck on UK courses…let's go abroad…

How about the aptly named (Jack Nicklaus designed) Valhalla in Louisville Kentucky, a mere 7115 yards par 72 (apparently private membership costs approximately $45,000). Then there's a little bit of heaven on earth at SunRidge Canyon Golf Club in Fountain Hills, Arizona with cacti, gullies, the Sonoran desert and 6823 yards of carefully deliberated planning and design walking hand-in-hand with nature.

Off to the Portuguese Algarve and there's nothing to compare with the magic of San Lorenzo (although Valderrama and Estoril get a lot of points). In Paris, Jimmy Tarbuck selects Morfontaine, or, when in Spain, Atalaya Park (as long as the wild boar haven't dug up the greens).

Whether, like me, you find yourself on top of the world in the land down under (Australia), jamming in Jamaica, snorkelling in the Seychelles, singing in Singapore, basking in Bali, mesmerised in Manzanillo, moody in Marbella, feeling grand in Rio or fluttering in the Bahamas, there's a string of courses hiding away just waiting for you to go out and discover them. Be friendly, diplomatic and keen (have your handicap card with you) and chances are you'll get your round, but please remember…when you are abroad you are an ambassador for the players of your country who wish to follow you to that course!

C is for Competition...

Let's not get into the Johnnie Walker Classic, the Heineken Classic, Apollo Week, South African PGA Championship, Dubai Desert Open, Portuguese Open, Cannes Open, Italian Open, B&H International Open, Scottish Open, Sun Dutch Open, Volvo Masters, Loch Lomond World Invitational, Alfred Dunhill Cup, Canon European Masters, Mercedes Championship, Bob Hope Chrysler Classic, Las Vegas Invitational, Sara Lee Classic, Samsung World Championship, Toray Japan Queen's Cup, Austrian Ladies Open, Welsh Open, McDonald's WPGA, the LPGA Championship, Honda Classic…

Notes

C is for Competition

From January through to November (maybe even December in places) there seems to be a world-class championship tournament in play somewhere in the world. The worldwide status of golf these days attracts some hefty sponsors and the prize money can be extremely attractive with purses well into the millions. It's the closest thing I can think of to that pot of gold at the end of the rainbow.

Since 1920 it seems, when the Glasgow Herald offered a £650 top prize and the following year sponsored the Glasgow Herald £1000 Guineas Tournament, international players of distinction have gathered together to slam it out for the glittering prizes. On offer, amongst others, the Walker Cup, the Open Championship and perhaps the best known of all, the Ryder Cup. Ask anyone, whether or not they play, to name a competition to do with golf and they'll most probably know of the Ryder Cup, named after it's founder Samuel Ryder.

D is for Divots...

These are rather small pieces of turf carved by the clubface out of the ground in the process of making a stroke, which should be replaced by the player.

Speaking of divots, did you hear about the fanatical fan who followed the circuit watching his hero for year after year, always carrying a large shoulder bag? It transpires that he always collected the divots his hero knocked out on the course, which he faithfully took home until he had an entire lawn constructed only of divots. I don't believe this is an apocryphal story and for some reason Arnold Palmer springs to mind (I could be wrong) as the pro the fan was following. Anyway, it puts a new slant to the term stalking.

D is for Debut...

The Chemapol Czech Open (August 1996) had a pleasant surprise or two for followers of tennis. Champion player Ivan Lendl made his debut on the professional golf circuit and, what's more, he played left-handed, which is curious as he is a right-handed tennis player.

Notes

D is for Drive...
See also Woods

What do you focus on when you drive? Here's a trick I've seen used by many successful players. Instead of focusing on the whole ball, try to concentrate on just the rear section of the ball and see what that does for your contact. For some players this really helps.

D is for Duffer...

What does the keen 'duffer' want for Christmas? Yes, a golf bag. Not just a bag, but an entire miniature world that, if captured by an alien who happened accidentally to select a duffer as representative of mankind, would send him packing back to his planet of origin with a recommendation never again to contemplate rational communication with human beings. These, he would conclude, all have their own shoulder-carried (or trolley-wheeled) environment in which lives various-shaped gloves (some with and some without fingers), a selection of strange-looking long metal objects with funny heads, balls, different coloured tees, markers, pencils, hip flask, club socks, spare socks, towels, umbrella, sun hat, rain hat, sunglasses, and most probably a mobile phone and a box of cigars! It's a far cry from the inspirational image of a couple of bearded, elderly Scotsmen crossing the Glens of Scotland knocking a small object through the heather to pass the time as they walked for miles actually to get somewhere!

Notes

Notes

E is for Eagle...

Or two under par on a hole. (Par is the number of strokes assigned to a hole.) So, work it out for yourself ...say you achieve an eagle on a par five hole. How many strokes did it take you?

E is for Electric trolley...

Two players observe a man running in the distance.

1st golfer: Since when did they allow joggers onto the course?

2nd golfer: That's not a jogger, it's Smith trying to catch his new electric trolley!

Notes

E is for Etiquette...

Whatever level of prowess you have achieved, all golfers have one thing in common to adhere to and that is golfing etiquette. This covers everything from safety and consideration of other players, who has priority on the golf course, the use of golfing carts, replacing divots, raking bunkers, repairing ball-marks and so forth. Before splashing out on expensive new kit and dashing off in your car to a course, it is advisable to acquaint yourself with the rules and etiquette of golf and probably the best guide is one of the official publications of the Royal & Ancient Golf Club of St Andrews, such as *Golf Rules Illustrated.* If after reading through the contents you still feel like golfing, you will at least not feel awkward on the course and will have some idea of what's going on and expected of you.

E is for Equipment...

A golfer came staggering back to the locker room looking obviously distressed. The pro, recognising the member, came over to him and placed his hand on his shoulder. 'Whatever is wrong, Jack?' asked the pro with genuine concern in his voice. Jones looked up at his friendly face and sobbed, 'I've just accidentally killed my wife on the first tee,' he explained.

'Killed your wife! How?' asked the pro.

'I was trying out my new driver and didn't see her there behind me as I took a back swing. I hit her on the head and she fell to the ground...stone dead!' he described. The pro paused to think for a moment and then broke the silence.

'What club were you using?' he asked the man.

'It was my brand new Burner Bubble driver!' he explained, still sobbing.

'Great club!' came the pro's reply.

'Yes, on my next shot I cracked an enormous 284 yards drive straight down the centre of the fairway!'

Notes

F is for Fakes...

The marketplace today is flooded with counterfeit products designed to help you look the part for a fraction of the cost, whether it's perfume or jewellery or clothing. But we all know what happens. The fake Rolex turns your wrist green and, whereas the authentic Fred Perry shirt will give you years of faithful service and still look smart, the illegal fake will go tatty in the wash. And the same goes for equipment. Look out for counterfeit golf clubs. You might think you're getting a bargain with a set of clubs that looks just as good as the better-known, genuine make, but rest assured, it's likely the fake didn't get taken through the mill to iron out its performance flaws before going into production. You're most likely to be paying for looks rather than performance. Clubs with a branded name (your pro shop will help you out) have been designed carefully, exhaustively tested and perfected and, although perhaps a little bit more money, they'll provide you with long and faithful service. You owe it to yourself not to fall into the trap of succumbing to the fake.

F is for 'Feel the need'...

When you pack your bag, have a long look at what you're carrying. Do you really need all those long-game clubs? You've probably got a 1 and 2 iron in there and two or three different woods. Are you likely to use them? How about shedding some weight – and think of the short game too. What's useful? Certainly a pitching wedge and a sand wedge, maybe a 9 iron (useful on a downhill approach) and some canny players will carry another wedge with some additional loft.

F is for Five iron... '5'

Y̲ou've landed on the fringe of the green, so try your less lifted 5 iron and your putting grip with a slow and even swing, almost a putting action. The 5 should get you onto the green and, if you aim at the flag, you might get down.

Notes

F is for Fourteen clubs...

What clubs do you need to get successfully round the course and score well? Here's a caddy's suggestion. You can do it with only a 3 wood, a 5, 7 and 9 iron, your sand wedge and putter. This is a good basic set, of course you can carry up to your maximum fourteen clubs but then think of all those decision you're going to have to make along the way.

G is for Golf...

Golf has come a long long way since the romantic image of a couple of Scottish gentlemen knocking a haggis, or whatever it was, across the Glens. Nowadays, from motorised club trolleys to personally inscribed tees and balls, golf carts as impressive as sports cars, to the clubs you'd kill to get membership of, golf is an enjoyable discipline with no shortcut to success. A better umbrella won't make you a better golfer…but you can!

G is for Golf...

The origins of the game are unclear. Some say it comes from the old Scottish word *gouf,* which has a variety of spellings. Then there are those who believe the Scots borrowed the game from the Dutch who had a word *kolf* (or colf)…indeed, the Dutch had a game resembling golf which, according to some sources, was called 'game played with a club' or *spel metten kolven.* Just to complicate matters further, the Romans had a game which they named *paganica* and played with a leather ball stuffed with feathers but, just un petit moment, mes amis! The French had a game called *jeu de mail* based on a club and ball and scored in strokes. I, of course, think that, as soon as man was trying to get on his feet with the aid of a stick, he soon began to become independent of the stick and, from that moment, began knocking objects about with it in a nonchalant manner to break the monotony of the new found mode of travel – walking upright!

G is for Golf...

This much is certain. There is a stained glass window in Gloucester Cathedral showing a golfer which must date from at least the 14th century. James II of Scotland banned golf in 1457 because no work was getting done and Henry VIII's wife Catherine of Aragon is on record as being pleased with the game, which gives us the early 1500s. Never mind that the Dutch have traced back to 1300 a stick and ball game which incorporated an iron-headed club – anybody could have come up with that! But Scotland legitimised the game by devising and publishing the rules of golf. Not only that, but the 19th hole would never be the same were Dutch chocolate or creme de menthe served in place of 'a wee doch'-an-do'ris' (a quaint, internationally famous Scottish cordial), now would it!

Notes

Notes

G is for the Golden Bear...

Jack Nicklaus, the 'Golden Bear', and outstanding golfer at his height still met with his old teacher Jack Grout prior to competitions to get a complete refresher course in all the basics and to make sure he wasn't straying off the track.

G is for the Great White Shark...

Greg Norman's No 1 grass strain (see next entry) matches his own deserved ranking as world's No 1. He had probably the worst luck any golfer could imagine possible in April 1996 during the Masters. It was the sort of misfortune that, no matter how many millions you had in the bank, in sporting terms could brand itself into your psyche for a long, long time to come and would perhaps ruin any lesser mortal. Greg was third round leader, having ended the first round on an equal course record of 63. At the end of the second round he was six shots up on the rest of the field, but (cue the music) nightmare of nightmares, he suffered four consecutive bogeys and found himself level with Nick Faldo at the 12th. Then, as all great sharks do, I suppose, Greg found water! Can you imagine how he felt that day? He began six shots ahead of Nick Faldo and ended the round five shots behind him. The British press unkindly renamed Greg the 'Great White Fish Finger'.

Notes

G is for Greg's grass...

The Great White Shark Greg Norman has taken his golf right back to the roots. Grass roots in fact. Greg's business empire has been busy cultivating a new strain of Bermuda grass which he's named GN1. It's a huge success and baseball and football teams all over America have placed their orders. Samuel Ryder himself made his packet from seeds and it was the great Walter Hagen who said, 'Never hurry, never worry and always remember to smell the flowers on the way.'

G is for Grip...

L et's think about the grip for a moment. It's important to get the correct grip or nothing will ever come right. What we're trying to achieve on the golf course is a moment when the club-face is square to the ball target line. Now you can invest in getting this right by purchasing what is called a 'practice grip', which you can fit onto a club to get used to holding it correctly. You won't be allowed to use it in competition so it's only there to help your 'body memory' record what it should be doing.

Or you can try to set it up, remembering that what you should end up with is the left hand wrapped comfortably but securely around the club, with the left thumb running down the front of the shaft. This is easily formed by starting with your left arm hanging naturally at your side. Then, wrap your right hand around it and your right thumb will cover most of your left thumb, running slightly left of it. Look at the V formed between your thumb line and forefinger. It should point at your chin and you should only be able to see at most about a knuckle and a half on your left hand. This will ensure the club-face comes square on and the ball 'should' be propelled straight along the ball target line.

It's important not to grip the club too tightly and make sure your hands are parallel. Do not let the grip loosen during the swing or the club will move and the face will not arrive square. If the face arrives closed, your ball will fly left, but club-face open, ball goes right! Hit some balls and adjust the point of the V left or right until you find the combination that marries your swing and gives you a straight flight!

G is for Grip...

S ome people still play using a grip that would conform to the old-fashioned St Andrews style, which included no overlocking and no overlapping of fingers. I think its official name is the ten-finger grip but I've also heard it referred to as the palm grip or the 'baseball' grip. I haven't had a straight answer to this one from anybody, although, in a fabulous book by Jack Nicklaus about the swing, he uses the term ten-finger grip.

H is for Handicap...

When the handicapper gives you your handicap, don't worry, they're not going to injure you physically. It's a term, most probably borrowed from the sport of horse racing where, before the race they equal out the chances of all the horses and riders by adding extra weight to be carried by certain horses. In golf, though, it takes the form of a compensation in strokes assigned to players on the basis of their performance, recent past and current. This allows golfers of varied capabilities to compete together on what is considered to be as close to equal terms as any other system.

But be warned...you can be disqualified if you declare a higher handicap than you are entitled to as this will affect the number of strokes given or received. In stroke play you can also be disqualified for not recording your handicap on your scorecard before handing it in to the Committee.

H is for Heaven on Earth?

Back to Scotland, where the unique Findhorn Foundation near Forres in Moray are currently offering courses to explain the spiritual aspects of golf. For the not too outrageous fee of £550 (which includes green fees and professional tuition on some of Scotland's finest north-eastern courses) you too can participate over the week-long summer activity programme called 'Fairway to Heaven'. The Findhorn Foundation has already gained an impressive worldwide reputation for its work in organic farming, in which they are producing results most would consider impossible, as well as in meditation, yoga and alternative technology…Prince Charles is said to be extremely interested in their work…So, if you would like to get that heavenly shot, and improve your drive and your personal alignment by bringing the body and spirit into harmony, you'd better book early because, any outfit that can produce 40lb cabbages has the potential to send your golf ballistic!

Notes

H is for a bad case of Hives!
The Sting in the Tale

Caddie Artie Granfield had a lucky escape at the Tucson Open in 1996. He and Keith Fergus were attacked by an angry swarm of bees. Fortunately for Artie, he managed to dive into a lake but poor Keith suffered a lot of painful stings. Unless I'm very much mistaken, a similar thing happened to Jack Nicklaus and Gary Player in South Africa some time ago during an exhibition game they were playing. They had to abandon a hole after disturbing a swarm of killer bees and were seen withdrawing hastily, trying to stave off the attack with golf towels, to pick up the game further along the course. So Bee Careful!

I is for Inspiration...

So golf has been around for centuries and is constantly evolving to its next dimension with the introduction of new and (sometimes) better technological breakthroughs which result in newer equipment, lighter clubs, faster balls, cooler clothing, squeakless trolleys…you name it. But, interestingly, the basics of effective golf have remained pretty much the same for decades and perhaps the most fundamental thing for any golfer to achieve is a good, consistent swing. It doesn't surprise me to find that players today take their lead from golfers of 60 years or so ago – and why not? If it worked for them and fits your own rhythm, why not adopt it? The 'inspired' golfer doesn't always play the best golf but at least they enjoy themselves, which, if you're not on the tour and after the glittering prizes, is the most important aspect to the game.

There are volumes upon volumes that take the reader through every single feature of the game and focus on the minutiae of every aspect until the head rings and the body seizes up with anxiety. It doesn't mean you shouldn't read a good golf book by a pro whose achievement and innovation can be monitored through success (and informed failure, which is equally as important). But what I have observed is that there is no one single way of pulling it off. So, and I'll be lynched by the purists for this but I'll say it anyway because I honestly believe it:

'If it works for you, use it!'

I is for Irons...

Golf has come a long way since the heady romantic days of clubs with names like heavy iron, track iron, driving cleek, mashie, spade mashie, sammy, rake, president, putting cleek, brassie, jigger, iron niblick, bunker iron (also called sand iron), lofting iron and mid-iron. Now you can get closer to the pin with your Fatboy, drive with your Controller, putt with your Teardrop, fill your bag with names like Ping, Burner Bubbles, Zebras, and Big Bertha. Chances are that your prized iron is constructed of the newest materials such as titanium, graphite, stronomic and aluminium. There are a number of pros on the tour who can get round using a single iron to complete every shot and still score well. Wherever possible with irons, or any clubs you are considering buying, ask to use their 'trial' club to see how it performs rather than buying blind. The course is not the place to discover your mistake!

Notes

Notes

J is for Jacklin...

Britain (and Europe) have a lot to be grateful for and at the top of the golfing 'thank you' list has got to be the great Tony Jacklin. Tony had long been emerging as star material in British golf when he became instantly famous via television coverage of the Dunlop Masters. At the 16th he holed in one in a brilliant shot and the whole world gasped. Even mums of brothers of friends whose 'friends were golfers' were talking about it for weeks. Jacklin left Royal St George's the winner, completing the final round on 64. It certainly put him into the British team in 1967 for the Ryder Cup. He eventually went on to become our Ryder team captain and brought long-awaited victory back to Europe.

J is for Jokes...

W hy are you looking so pleased with yourself? the pro quizzed the man in the locker room.

'It was our tenth wedding anniversary and I got a new set of golf clubs for my wife,' came his reply.

'A new set of golf clubs for your wife? That's the best trade I've ever heard of!'

Then there was the case of two women playing a round of golf together. On the ninth green one of the women misses the putt and mutters something under her breath. It so happens it is exactly the reaction the other woman's husband comes out with under exactly the same circumstances...the secret love affair is out of the bag!

Notes

Notes

K is for Keep your Eye on the Ball!
I've heard of solutions to wet weather but this takes the cake.

One of my favourite comedians, Tom O'Connor, apparently plays wearing contact lenses and, because his eyes are equally short-sighted he wears one lens in his right eye for driving and the other lens in his left eye is for putting.

K is for Keeping up Appearances...

As it dangerously neared their tee-off time, three players waited anxiously by their cars, which were all parked side by side in the car park of their swanky club. The banker was beside his immaculate Mercedes, the dentist leaned against his Porsche and the media man was tying up his shoe lace on the bumper of his new Bentley. Just then arrived their fourth player in a smoking old Lada with a slipping clutch. He jerkily parked the car next to theirs and jumped out all set for the off.

'Sorry I'm late, fellows,' he called chirpily.

'It really isn't on, you know, parking a car like this out here. It lets down the club…creates a bad impression,' said the banker.

'That's okay,' said the man, 'I've got £70,000 worth of diamonds in the boot!'

Notes

Notes

L is for Lessons...

Invest a very small amount of money in something you will benefit from for the rest of your playing life. A couple of lessons with a pro and preferably one who knows your game. You'll wonder why you never thought of it before. In just a short time a professional helps you imprint your body language with enough of the 'right way' to go about things to have a really positive effect on your playing.

L is for Love life...

In a somewhat embarrassed manner a male patient confided to his GP that he was having trouble at home… with sex, with his wife.

'I just don't seem to be able to…' he went on with difficulty.

'There, there, dear fellow,' said his doctor. 'You're a little overweight and unfit, which doesn't help at all. I want you to take some exercise. Here, take my spare set of golf clubs and let me know how you get on.'

The man thanked the doctor, and left his surgery carrying the clubs. When the doctor hadn't heard from him for over six months he decided to ring him at home.

'Hello, Doc. I can't thank you enough for what you've done for me,' said the obviously delighted patient.

'So your love life with your wife has returned to normal?' the doctor asked.

'Oh, that. No, we got divorced – but my golf's coming along marvellously. My handicap's down to 6!'

Notes

Notes

M is for Married golfers...

If you're a married male golfer, try this. Tell your partner that you think she is a wonderful poet. That way, on a Sunday morning when the weather's nice and you're getting dressed for a game of golf, she will open the curtains and say, 'Lo, the morn!' – instead of telling you to get out of your golf shoes to go, 'Mow the lawn!'

Notes

M is for Mature...

How is it that Jack Nicklaus, now just past the mid-50s mark, is still capable of driving the ball so far? Is it just me or is the Golden Bear suddenly hitting drives like he used to years ago? 'Is it monkey glands?,' I hear you ask. Or, could it have anything to do with his new driver? His golfing equipment company has made him an 'Air Bear' which is longer and lighter than his past drivers, has a slightly larger head and utilises titanium technology. If his consistent extra 30 plus yards is anything to go by, this is going to be the driver they all cry out for.

M is for Midnight sun...

Did you hear about the many times divorced Icelandic golfer who, in desperation married an unsuspecting English woman. He explained to her, 'It is the custom here, that after the wedding ceremony, the men go out for the rest of the day to play golf and return when it gets dark to consummate the marriage.' She smilingly agreed, so off he went and was gone between the middle of March until the beginning of November!

Notes

N is for Nassau...

Nassau is responsible for sending more than rockets into orbit. I deal a little with wagering later on, but beware the player who invites you to play a £50 Nassau. This quaint little term, already in use at the beginning of the 1900s, can cost you dear in the end. You will be laying an equal stake wager on the first nine holes, the second nine holes and the whole round! It could well be the root of the expression 'being stung three ways'.

Notes

N is for Nature...

Golf is also a wonderful way of getting into contact with nature. The excellent pro-celebrity player, comedian Tom O'Connor, once pointed out to me the fact that, although trees are made up of over 90 per cent water, you shouldn't expect to hear a 'splash' when your ball hits one!

Notes

Notes

Never mind yer Niblick...N is for Nineteenth hole!

No bunkers, or dog-legs, water hazards or ground under repair here. No rabbit scrapes, ruts, rough or raving. The friendliest of holes and a veritable reservoir, a positive oasis for the celebrating or lamenting golfer alike. It is of course the bar at the golf club. A most popular hole! Cheers…

Notes

O is for Out of Bounds!

This, rather like that distance between enemy trenches during the war, is a no-man's land usually either side (or variations to this) of the fairway. If it's marked by a fence or stake markers, then the inside edges are out of bounds. If marked with a line then even the line is out of bounds if you land on it. Although you can stand out of bounds to play a ball still within bounds, the reverse does not apply. If your ball is out of bounds it is prohibited to play it. (See the R&A rules about ball in play and playing a provisional ball. I'd give the full rulings here but that would be out of bounds.)

P is for Partners and Planning...

When you are playing with a partner try to make your plans in advance of the tee. There's nothing more offputting than a running debate on the course. Play a two-ball foursome and get used to playing for each other. You concentrate not on your individual ability to go for a birdie but, instead, make certain you place the ball in the best possible position for your partner to take the next shot – it's quick and effective. On the green get that ball close and well laid to the hole for your partner to knock down…partner line-up and partner follow-through. Swap order from time to time. It's a very good method of preparing for team golf too. If you need to get the big swings out of your system, knock out some practice balls before you tee off, but not too many or you'll exhaust yourself before you begin. Go for precision not exhibition!

P is for Practice...

There is a wonderful old game designed to cheer up a long day and which allows you to get in some good putting practice. It is known as Clock Golf. Arrange some cut-out numbers like those found on a clock face on your own back lawn. Lay them out in such a way that the hole is off centre, which will allow different putting distances from each number when they are laid out in a circle. So, you have your clock. Players, or teams of players, take it in turn to putt from each of the numbers and keep the score. The game lasts until you have been right around the clock and the winners will have taken the lowest total of putts for all twelve putting points. The nice thing is that you can keep altering the position of the numbers so it needn't ever become boring and even the least proficient golfer amongst you will find themselves a few moments of glory!

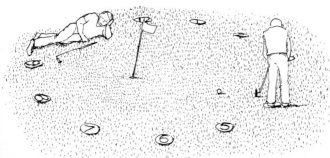

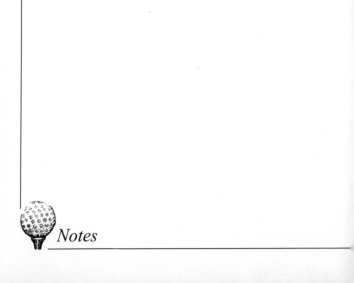

Notes

P is for Putting...

On the subject of putting and how easy it is to have your concentration broken, P G Wodehouse, who gave us so many excellent golfing moments in his various writings, had this to say in *The Unexpected Clicking of Cuthbert:*

'The least thing upset him on the links. He missed short putts because of the uproar of butterflies in the adjoining meadows.'

Notes

Notes

Q is for Quiz...

Quiz 1

Do you know who's being described here? Picked up the Mercedes championship trophy in January 1997, the most successful amateur since Jack Nicklaus, turned pro only six months before, three major wins in nine events since August 1996, already won over $1m in prize money, is reported to have over $60m in endorsements. Tom Watson has described this player as being, 'the most important golfer in the last 50 years'.

(Answer at back of book)

Q is for Quiz...

Quiz 2

What are the following?

Baffy-spoon
Bail out
Croquet
Dog-leg
Double-bogey
Flange
Galleryite
Hog-back
Pill
Rake

(Answers at back of book)

Notes

R is for Range...

B efore you go running off to the driving range, talk
yourself out of the temptation to grab your driver
immediately and start bashing out huge unco-ordinated
drives all over the place. You will be surrounded by activity,
balls flying every which way and beside you will be a bucket
of balls. Work up to the driver. Target your shots. Try to
achieve a consistency and don't rush between shots. You're
there to get information about your game, so don't waste the
opportunity. Some driving ranges have fixed rubber tees to
play off. You have to work out whether these match the way
you play on the course. If they don't, see if you can use a tee
peg, but most pros would say, if you can't, don't
compromise. Concentrate on other shots and leave the
driving until another time.

R is for Reading about golf...

Reading about golf is about as important as the skills and techniques involved in playing it. Why? Because in practically everything you read you'll come up against some incident or fact that could affect your own future game. For example, it would be good to know that, if you search for the ball you lost for over ten minutes, you will be subject to a penalty for undue delay!

Go to your video shop, library or bookstore and search out the writings of these and other greats: Jack Nicklaus, Tony Jacklin, Arnold Palmer, Sam Snead, Ben Hogan, Billy Casper, Walter Hagen, Lee Travino, Tom Watson, Peter Alliss, Seve Ballesteros, Sandy Lyle, Peter Oosterhuis, Sam Torrance. Tune in to what's happening as it happens through the various monthly magazines on golf and get out there and be a part of it.

R is for Recipe for disaster...

Then there was the time a ball from the women's four was being held up by three men on the green ahead of them, the men were debating wildly with arms flailing about and raised voices. On closer inspection one of the women discovered that they were infact the three amateur chefs arguing about the correct moment to add the cream to a steak au poivre!

Notes

Notes

R is for Repetition...

Don't experiment on the golf course! It's the worst place. Try the practice tee or a driving range. You can't keep changing things on the course from shot to shot and expect things to work out for you. Watch many overzealous-amateurs and you'll notice after two holes that you're watching an erratic game. Follow a pro or a seasoned amateur and you'll soon observe the amount of repetition involved in good golf.

R is for Rivalry...

I magine the scene – two golfers, old rivals...So much so that, although they looked forward to their regular rounds together, they had given up speaking to each other years ago. They drive off on the 17th hole. One walks ahead to the ball sitting on the edge of the green and the other, cursing loudly, climbs into the sand trap where he takes five shots to play out. The ball flies over the green and into another trap on the other side of it. He swears loudly and crosses to that trap to play it out. Four swings and the ball is airborne but lands back in the first sand trap. This happens several times until the air becomes blue with expletives. Then his partner comes in. 'Do you mind if I point something out to you, old man?' he says calmly.

'What the —k could you —king tell me that's of any —king use, you smug old —ard?' came the angry response.

His rival grinned slightly and said, 'You appear to be playing my ball'.

R is for Round...

There's a lovely gag attributed to Alistair Cooke. It's about a man who had an absolutely terrible round of golf. It was so bad, in fact, that he slit his wrists with a cut-throat razor. When they had been bandaged, he staggered into the locker room and asked his partner, 'What time shall we play tomorrow?'

Notes

Notes

R is for Rules the waves!

Can you define, clearly, the difference between a 'water hazard' and 'casual water' and the players' options?

R is for Ruling...

There was an incident on the ninth hole at Gleneagles. A man rushed to the hotel and said, 'Doctor, come quickly!' which he did. Eventually they reached the place where a small circle of men were bent over the scene of the incident. 'Let me through', said the doctor, only to find a golf ball, not a person, was the centre of all the attention. 'So, doctor, is it or is it not a rabbit scrape?'

Notes

R is for Ruling...

W hat would you do?

Anyone following the 1996 Volvo PGA Championship at Wentworth will have shared in the predicament which faced Nick Faldo on the 17th in the second round. Faldo hit his second shot and it was heading out of bounds, then it hit a tree, bounced back towards the green but came to rest 'on' a spectator's bag! Nick felt he should mark the spot on the grass where the ball would have come to rest, lift the ball, remove the bag and then place the ball.

Even when the rules official attended the scene there was confusion as he said that Faldo should drop the ball not place it. Can you work out what should be done in such a situation?

(Answer next page)

So how did you get on with your ruling? Place or drop?

If your ball lies *in* or *on* a movable obstruction you mark its position and then drop the ball. If the ball comes to rest *against* a movable obstruction, then you move the obstruction and replace the ball. (See the R&A rule 24-.)

The Wentworth outcome of Faldo's predicament was reported by Alistair Tait for the excellent magazine *Golf Monthly,* August 1996:

'Where the official was wrong in Faldo's case was that the ball was closer to the hole when dropped both times. Each time the official told Faldo the ball was in play, but Faldo stuck to his guns and insisted on eventually placing the ball on the correct spot.'

R is for Ruling...

Did you know that if you are playing in a 36 hole match then you are entitled to change your golf clubs after the first 18 holes? See your rule book.

Notes

R is for Ruling...

No, you can't ask the distance between your ball in play and the hole on the putting green...it would be taking 'advice'. However, if you work out how far you are from the tree on your right, you are allowed to ask how far the tree is from the hole...that would not be 'advice' because the tree is a permanent object.

Ruling Quiz

Test yourself. You are on the teeing ground and there is grass growing behind the ball. Are you allowed to pull out or break off the grass?

(Answer at back of book)

Notes

R is for the Ryder Cup...

Probably the most dynamic and thrilling competition in the world is the Ryder Cup. (Thank you, Samuel Ryder.) Since 1926 the Ryder Cup has signalled the emergence of some exceptional talent and heart-stopping moments. Like the 1969 contest in which Tony Jacklin and Jack Nicklaus tied the contest. Or how, after years of American domination, the tables turned in 1985 when, under the captaincy of the superb Tony Jacklin, the Europeans beat the USA, something the Americans had not experienced since 1957 thanks to players including Jack Nicklaus, Sam Snead, Ben Hogan, Arnold Palmer and Jimmy Menaret. If the 1960s gave Britain and Europe a place on the map with music and fashion, the 1980s gave the same the likes of Sandy Lyle, Nick Faldo and the amazing Seve Ballesteros.

Notes

Notes

Notes

S is for Seven iron... '7'

You want to chip a shot over the apron to run on the green towards the flag? Try a low grip on a 7 iron for loft and make sure your backswing and throughswing are equal. Don't break at the wrist.

Notes

S is for Shot...

You've got one fundamental problem, Mr Jones. You
tend to stand too close to the ball, and that's after
you've hit it!

S is for St Andrews...

Did you know that you can go and play over the world-famous St Andrews links and tread in the footsteps of Nicklaus, Faldo, Ballesteros, Tom Morris and all those other greats? Seek out information about the Official St Andrew's Golf Week, a programme designed to improve your game whether or not you're an expert. Find out more and visit 'The Home of Golf' for yourself.

S is for Sand trap...

Here's an interesting piece of human character study...
Next time you come out of a sand trap in one and your
ball comes to rest only a foot or so from the pin, listen as
your opponent exclaims, 'Well played...great shot...' Watch
his face. The contradiction between the comment and the
facial expression is unique to golf.

Notes

Notes

S is for Slice!

There was the doctor who, because his friend and patient came to him suffering a bout of extreme depression, invited him to a round at his club. By the eighth hole the doctor took him aside and said, 'I've got some good news and some bad news. The good news is that you're not suffering clinical depression at all. The bad news is that what you have got is incurable.'

'What is it, doc?' the extremely concerned fellow asked.

'Your slice!'

S is for Stableford...

There are many forms of competition but perhaps the most popular today is played to Stableford Rules, a system of scoring invented by Dr Frank Stableford way back in 1931. In this stroke competition, a player wins points in relation to fixed scores for each hole played. So, for example, a score of 1 point would be won for completing a hole one over par, 2 points for par, 3 points for one under par, 4 points for two under par and 5 points for three under par.

Notes

Notes

S is for Splash!

Have you ever used the expression 'splash out', perhaps saying to someone, 'Go on, why not splash out and buy something in the sales?' or similar? A splash shot is a good whack of the ball which takes it out from a rough lay, sand or high grass.

S is for Spectacular...

I t's taken Woosnam, Nicklaus, Norman and the other greats years to perfect their shots. Why is it that practically every recreational player feels compelled to pull off a spectacular shot? The best shot comes from the player who knows his or her strengths and sticks to them.

Notes

S is for Scots and Scotch...

Sometimes, in Scotland, at the best known of golf courses, guests might find themselves being greeted by a fully garbed bagpiper. One day, two extremely hungover guests who had yet to get over the supreme gala dinner from the night before, were off to face 18 wonderful holes. When they passed the piper, one remarked to the other:

'He's not got his pipes.'

'No,' replied his colleague, 'I borrowed them.'

'Why on earth did you do that? You can't play the bagpipes!'

'I know,' came his reply, 'And, as long as I've got them, neither can he!'

S is for Sayings...
Gimme that ding!

Kevin Costner's film Tin Cup was released during the writing of this book. His line that every golfer will by now have imprinted on their memories is:

'When you hit a good golf shot, a tuning fork rings in your loins!'

Notes

Notes

S is for Swing...

The Golden Bear – Jack Nicklaus – is reported as saying that the swing is an inexhaustible subject. This seems to be borne out by reading various pros' attempts to define it. You can also pick up good information from reading about the experiences of celebrities as they describe what they've come up against over various rounds and tournaments.

S is for Stress...

The idea is to try to remove as much of the stress and tension as possible. This is easily blown by a bad tee shot which never becomes as spectacular as intended and results in a poor lay, a tense second shot and a whole string of knock-on effects. Any strategic player will avoid this with a little bit of forward thinking and simply by playing within the boundaries of his or her own capabilities.

Notes

S is for Swing...

So what's my swing? Here's what works for me, allow some level of consistency and leave me happy with it. I have Tony Jacklin to thank for some of the imagery involved – and he's the better player, of course.

I stand and relax, side on to the target or hole. I look down at the ground, visualise a clock face on the ground and adjust myself until the imaginary hour hand is on the ten. I look back towards the target and get my leading shoulder just out of sight, then back at the clock and read 20 minutes after ten ...I look back at the target and make my distance. I challenge myself to be correct in my formulations by deciding the level of input to the shot and, if there's no wind (for which I would compensate in various minute movements around the clock) I put my home-made swing into action to bring the face through 20 minutes past ten to hit a spot smack in the middle of the back of the ball.

Of course, a pro would say I should imagine the line to run through the centre of my ball to the target, check the alignment of my upper body by holding a club across my chest from shoulder to shoulder, then see that the club runs parallel with the ball target line. That works too, but it's more difficult and less fun to adopt on the course.

Notes

S is for Sweet spot...

Every club has, hidden away on its face, what is known as the 'sweet spot'. It's the exact spot which gives the perfect hit, the best distance and 'sweetest' feel to the shot.

T is for Tip...

Here's something most of the better golfers do. If they aren't able to fit in a full practice session, they can be seen swinging a club for a few minutes a day. Each has their own agenda, of course, be it knocking the heads off dandelions or launching snowballs as if they were the real thing. The added confidence that a few practice swings gives them becomes clearly evident in their game when they get to the course, in contrast to the player who hasn't touched their clubs for several days or weeks. Try it. Chances are you'll start a trend in your area.

Notes

T is for Tip...

When the resident pro at the Belfry took me aside for some practice he made sure I concentrated first on hitting the ball hard and later we worked a little on control. I keep promising myself to carry on but I still hit a hard, uncontrolled ball that I can be proud of!

Notes

Notes

T is for Tip...

Another thing that separates the pro's and better amateurs from the 'duffers' is their ability to switch off thought at the right moments. A key moment, of course, is the swing, when the less going through your head the better. If you're standing at the tee and in your head you're saying to yourself, 'Keep your left arm straight…stay behind the ball…eye on the ball…elbow in…shoulders at 90 degrees… check grip…' etc, then you can bet your favourite driver sock that you're about to get it wrong!

T is for Tip...

Here's a tip from the top that will pay off on your game. When you go out for a walk, say along a country lane or through a park, try taking along a club and getting in a few practice swings along the way. In no time at all you'll experience the benefit to your game and you can knock down a few stinging nettles en route.

T is for Threesome...

Don't get confused by the term 'a threesome'. This is simply defined as three players in a match, one player against two. Each of the sides plays only one ball so, the side with two players takes alternate strokes with the same ball. Don't muddle this up with a 'three-ball', which is a match where all three play their own individual balls and each individual player is in competition with the two others.

T is for Tee...
Anyone for tee?

Teeing ground (starting place for the hole being played)

Tee up (place the ball on a tee, which is a small wooden or plastic peg)

Tee off (play a tee shot)

Tee shot (a shot played from a tee or teeing ground)

In the old days there used to be a box of sand available on the teeing ground expressly for the purpose of creating your tee!

Notes

T is for TEEth!

A man rushed into the dentist's surgery accompanied by his wife. By the look on his face he was suffering extreme anguish.

'Please,' the man begged of the dentist, 'you've got to help me. I need to have a tooth pulled out but I don't have time for an anaesthetic. I'm meeting an extremely important Japanese client on the golf course in half an hour and, if I'm late, I'll probably lose the deal.'

'It will hurt,' explained the dentist. 'Which tooth is it?' he asked the man.

The man turned to his wife and said, 'Show him which tooth is hurting you, darling!'

T is for Tops...

I f I had to single out the top male and top female players of the year for 1996 they would have to be, without a doubt, the totally unflappable Tom Lehman and Laura Davies. Tom's golf was an inspiration to us all, particularly the manner in which he won the 1996 Open. He certainly managed to keep his cool when the streaker appeared on the 18th and admitted in his victory speech that he preferred the female Wimbledon variety much better. Tom, who for all the world reminds me of Kevin Costner in his looks, appears like he's the guy they're all going to have to try and beat.

Laura, who carried a small television around the Evian Masters to watch the England vs Spain football match, has a winning combination working for her. It's a home-made swing, a sense of good fun, and a refusal to allow failures to affect her. It's certainly provided her with an enviable winning record and has carried her to the top whilst winning her a place in the history books for certain.

Notes

U is for Understanding...

It's pretty difficult to get much out of anything you don't understand. Take some time and get to know the quirks of the game, the rulings, the tools, and pretty soon you'll be into a world that's every bit as exciting as a great opera!

Notes

Notes

U is for the USPGA

This is the Professional Golfers' Association of America.

U is for Under Repair?

As if to frustrate the pants off an angel, there are certain rulings to do with Ground Under Repair which I have never been able to work out and doubtless hundreds of others share my angst! A fallen tree that is still attached to the stump is apparently not ground under repair but it can be deemed to be so by the Committee.

Even better, the lawnmower has been out and your ball has landed in a pile of fresh grass clippings that have been thrown under some bushes. Can you take a drop? No Way...because the clippings were thrown there to rot away so it's not ground under repair.

I wonder what happens when your ball lands on a shovel, in an icy puddle, over a shallow tractor rut, behind some cut firewood?

Notes

Notes

U is for Unplayable...

This is when the ball lands in a position where it's lie is fairly impossible to play out from. In this case the player can opt for 'relief' (that is, gaining permission under the rules to lift the ball and make a drop, in some cases incurring a penalty). See rules for guidance.

V is for Vardon...
I beg your pardon?

The overlapping grip as we know it is attributed to the
golfer Harry Vardon, apparently it was well in use
before he laid claim to it. Consensus is that he made it
fashionable and, as he was there playing brilliantly in the
first international way back in 1921, let's accept that Vardon
made it official.

Notes

Notes

V is for Visiting...

No matter where you are in the world, and whether or not you've come prepared with your own clubs, a round of golf is almost always available and needn't cost an arm and leg. If you're visiting a town in the UK, for example, simply ring the professional at the golf club and state your case. More often than not they'll accommodate visitors and even hire out the kit. If you're a bit shy, then try the concierge at your hotel who, without doubt, will be able to line up a game for you (just remember to leave a good tip). The one thing that would be worth having with you is your handicap or home club membership card. After all, it would be a pity to spend the rest of your life frustrated that you didn't even try to get onto the course of your dreams when you were staying just up the road from it and would never be back that way again…wouldn't it!

W is for Wager...

C an you make a wager? The R&A does not forbid such action, it seems. Their role is to protect the integrity of the game, those who play it and the rules governing professional and amateur status. Wagering between other individual players or teams participating in a game for enjoyment will not be deemed as prize money, although excessive gambling is usually frowned upon by any club.

Notes

Notes

W is for Waggle...

Now back to that little routine at the address. Volumes and volumes have been written on the 'waggle'. It is supposed to break the tension, help the concentration, allow the player to get the feel of the club, assess the feel of the club-head. But many have turned this moment of focusing into a full-scale ritualistic parade or dance. It is not impossible to catch a glimpse of players offering twenty or more waggles to the ball before employing their swing. The old Scots would coach as follows; 'So as ye waggle, so shall ye swing'. It would not surprise me to discover pros who can finance their new car on clinics designed to tackle only the issue of overabundance of waggling.

Notes

Notes

W is for wedges...

The irons that will give you the most loft are your wedges. (If you want to leap the hedges, the clubs to choose are wedges!) Ideal for those short chip shots over an obstacle when you use a slightly lower grip and a steep, positive downswing.

W is for Whiff...

What a whiff! Like its cousin, the air shot, the whiff is what the sound 'whiff' suggests, a stroke taken which entirely misses the ball. Many a topper will whiff a ball.

W is for Wildlife...

Two couples were one day playing a mixed foursome when the husband of one of the women had the misfortune to drive a perfect missile of a stroke clear down the fairway which landed on the head of an unsuspecting hare. Crack! The poor creature didn't stand a chance and down it fell. His wife's friend, judging from his shock at what he'd just done, said, 'Don't worry,' ran to the hare and sprayed it with an aerosol she produced from her golf bag. Immediately the hare jumped up and ran into the rough.

'That's incredible!' exclaimed the guilt-ridden golfer. What on earth was in that can?'

'Oh, nothing really…' replied the woman, 'It was only hair restorer!'

W is for Wind...

Here's something else you might like to try to help your game. Again, it's about being able to estimate.

Go down to the toy shop and buy some little toy gliders.

Take your squadron down to the park or a field – if you're lucky enough to have the space in your own garden all the better. Now stand still and let your senses take in the conditions. Is it hot or is it cold? Is there wind or a simple breeze and, if so, which direction is it blowing in?

Now fly your planes and see what happens. See if you can compensate for the breeze and get your plane near your target. Do you have to throw it a few yards right of target to allow the wind to bring it back on line? Eventually such momentary joyful absurdity will become useful to your game as the wind comes off the sea and you're going for the green!

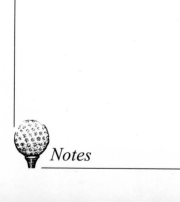

Notes

W is for Wodehouse...

PG Wodehouse was always keen to bring his pen to the subject of golf. There is a lovely passage in *There's Always Golf* which alludes to those players referred to as Tigers, or players of great strength. 'Plinlimmon is playing a nice game,' he said, 'nice and steady. Now that all the Tigers are off the map, I'm backing him.'

W is for Women in golf...

Will Laura land herself in the Hall of Fame alongside Nancy Lopez, Betsy King and Patty Sheehan? Of course, I'd wager!

Notes

W is for Women in golf...

In Europe Corrine Dibnah is probably the closest contender, certainly in career earnings but with only about half the tournament victories of Laura Davies. The mighty Annika Sorenstam has an impressive record and is getting better all the time. She won the US Women's Open for the second time in a row in 1996 and Laura was runner-up to her in the Betsy King LPGA Classic.

Notes

W is for Women...
Aussies far from down under!

Following in the limelight of Karrie Webb come Nadene Gole (winner of the 1996 Ford-Stimorol Danish Open) and Shani Waugh.

Notes

W is for Woods...

Let's take a little look at woods. If it's loft you're after, then a 5 wood will give it to you. Certainly more than your 3 wood, which will give you a little bit more distance. If it's really distance you're after then the longer-shafted 1 wood will get you there. So for height go for 5, for length go for 1.

Notes

W is for Wood driving...

Get someone to hold your wood for you and get down on your hands and knees and look at the ball on the tee in relation to the club-face. The ball should never have more or less than half of it above the top of the club face when the ball is addressed. So for your number 1 wood the tee peg is going to be higher than it will be with the 3 wood or 5 wood. If you have the tee too high and play your drive under the ball, you'll go into orbit. Too low against the club face and your shot will skim across the ground and travel a much shorter distance.

Notes

W is for Worship...

Ⓘt's a statistical fact that church attendances are proportionally up on Sundays where frost has closed the course. God works in mysterious ways!

Notes

X marks the spot...

The treasure lies at the bottom of the hole. All you've got to do is get there!

Y is for Yips...

You might be excused for thinking that on all golf courses there is a swarm of some new variety of mosquito-like insects called the 'yips'. They are regularly referred to and to be avoided at all costs. However, the 'yips' are in fact more a form of nervous spasm which can attack any player at any time, with a terrible effect upon their game. In Europe, certainly Britain, the better known term would be the 'twitch'. It might be a certain club or every time one is faced with a dog-leg, or worst of all perhaps is on the green. The annoying factor being that the harder one seems to fight to control the anxiety of getting a case of the 'yips', the more likely they are to attack and the player is to 'yip' a putt off the green!

Y is for Yips...

Yips? It was apparently that wonderful champion Sam
Snead who said that he'd rather see a rattlesnake than a
two-foot downhill putt with a break.

Y is for YOU!

So, whatever your level of prowess, golf has something for you and you will have something to bring to the game. As with all activities, it's good to be inspired and there are certainly enough exciting players around today to get your blood racing. Who can watch Greg Norman, Nick Faldo, Ian Woosnam (particularly if you can track down the photo of him at Sun City in 1987 holding up a 4 foot cheque for $1,000,000.000!), Laura Davies and the entire string of players on the tours today and not be thrilled?

Notes

Notes

Z is for Zealot...

O kay, everyone who's anyone in golf has written their training book, promising to pass on their method and to give you everything you need to become a champion yourself. So here's the basis for a whole new methodology which can work for you...

A few things might seem to have nothing at all to do with golf, but try them and tell me honestly that, besides seeming a little strange to do at first, they don't help to shape your game and independence as a player.

Baird's Supplementary Off-Course Training for Golfers

Lesson one

Take out a pen and a piece of paper.

Draw two small dots on the page – one somewhere on the bottom and the other somewhere near the top. Now, using your pen, draw a line from the bottom dot which is as straight as possible and which joins it to the top dot.

Done that? Okay.

Now estimate the length of the line and write down your answer on the page.

All finished? Good. Now get out a ruler and check how straight the line you drew was and confirm the distance between the two.

How did you get on? Try it several times – bigger lines can be done on a newspaper. Eventually…go out into your garden or the park and take a builder's tape measure with you.

Notes

Lesson two

So you're outside now with your tape measure.

Take some stones or sticks with you. Stand very still and visualise a spot you would like to reach and then, with a swing of the arm, try to pitch your object to that point. Have a few goes until you are satisfied with the landing.

Now, from the point you are at, try to estimate the distance to the point where you're best shot landed and then check it with the tape measure.

A re you beginning to understand the reasoning behind this bizarre methodology? The idea is to develop your hand, eye and brain skills until you can estimate the distance you are attempting to cover and the amount of energy likely to be needed to reach your target. It will help you out there on the course.

Lesson three

This is to take what you've been doing out in nature and try to translate it to your use of golf equipment.

Go to some fields or common ground (if this is not available, miss a step and head for the nearest driving range). Try the same exercise. Visualise the target and spend time developing a comfortable and consistent method of reaching it with club and balls. On the range distances will be indicated, but in nature you can guess, then stride it out to check how near you were.

This game will help your body to accept the other more technical aspects of swing etc. as body instinct and they should eventually become second nature. While your opponent is standing there waggling, thinking the swing through, running through the physical checklist and worrying whether or not it's going to be a whiff he produces, you will be enjoying the game at a moment that has intent. The rest is body impulse!

Notes

The Last Hole

I leave you with one final consideration. Spare a thought for the player who was so desperate about her poor golfing average that she went to the doctor. She was instructed to play a round, but only with the ball, not with a club of any sort. The idea was to imagine the shots and record her scores on her card. She did it and returned to the doctor who read her card. 'Good scores,' said the doctor, 'Try the same thing tomorrow but this time with a club but no ball and, again, keep your scores.' So she did and returned to the doctor in very good spirits.

'Excellent scores', said the doctor. 'How do you feel now?'

'Pretty good', said the patient.

'Then my advice to you is this. You should give up golf while your scores are good and you're ahead!'

Answer to Quiz 1
Who was being described? American junior champion at 15 and today with the world at his fingertips, he is, of course, Tiger Woods.

Answers to Quiz 2
Baffy-spoon No longer in use, this was a short, stiff wooden club with a spooned face used mainly for approach shots until iron play through the green was introduced.

Bail out Means to improve a bad start to a hole, either with some extremely good putting or a good approach shot.

Croquet Mainly a putting term associated with a stance resembling someone holding a croquet mallet. Much frowned upon until banned in 1968.

Dog-leg A hole with a fairway incorporating a sharp turn, ie, a dog-leg to the right or left.

Double-bogey Two strokes over par for a hole.

Flange The part that projects from the back of an iron club-head.

Galleryite   One of the spectators at a golfing match or tournament. En masse, they are referred to as a gallery.

Hog-back   Ridge of ground or a ridge on the fairway.

Pill   Ball.

Rake   Was a club used for playing out of sand or from water. It had vertical slots or prongs where the face would normally be.

Answer to Ruling Quiz
Are you allowed to pull out or break off the grass growing behind the ball on the teeing ground? Yes.

Published by MQ Publications Ltd
254-258 Goswell Road, London EC1V 7EB

Copyright © MQ Publications Ltd 1997

Text © David Baird 1997
Illustrations © Anny Evason 1997

ISBN: 1-897954-88-3

Printed and bound in Hong Kong